2/28/11

To Bill & Susan)

"Hope This helps you to
communicate better with
each other and learn to be
kind to each other "

all the best,

Rich Steve

Dr. Blues' Guide to
Making Relationships Work

Dr. Blues' Guide to Making Relationships Work
50 Quick Tips That Will Save Your Relationship

Manufactured in China.

For information, please contact:
Brown Books Publishing Group
16200 North Dallas Parkway, Suite 170
Dallas, Texas 75248
www.brownbooks.com
972-381-0009
A New Era in Publishing™

ISBN-13: 978-1-933285-66-5
ISBN-10: 1-933285-66-4
LCCN: 2006933115
1 2 3 4 5 6 7 8 9 10

Dr. Blues' Guide to
Making Relationships Work

50
Quick Tips
That Will Save Your
Relationship

Richard Blue, PhD

BROWN BOOKS
PUBLISHING

Lisa Blue, PhD, JD

This book was written to empower you to stop and think about positive ways to improve the quality of your relationship. A ready reference of tips, including descriptions and examples of the wrong way and the right way to handle situations, our book provides small steps you can take to change the way you relate to your partner. It gives you the tools to become proactive and commit to strengthening your bond. Remember, even a minor change in a positive direction is significant. Start by focusing on one tip, and watch as your small effort yields big rewards.

Intro

RECOGNIZE WHAT THE OTHER PERSON *Does Right*

THE WRONG WAY

- Find fault with and criticize the other person.
- Express your frustration in ways that make the other person feel devalued.
- Use a tone of voice that is critical and condescending.

THE RIGHT WAY

- Show appreciation for the little things the other person does.
- Verbalize positive comments to your partner on a daily basis.
- Remember that no one is perfect, and no one can meet all of your expectations. Focus on the other person's positive behaviors, and give negative feedback in a way that is not offensive. Be nice!

DEVELOP [Empathy] FOR THE OTHER PERSON

THE WRONG WAY

- Think that your way of looking at a situation is the only way.
- Believe that the other person is wrong when he or she verbalizes a viewpoint opposite of your own.
- Develop the attitude that the other person must always agree with you.

THE RIGHT WAY

- Acknowledge that everyone has the right to see the world through his or her own filter.
- Realize that you can disagree with the other person's viewpoint and still respect it.
- Actively listen in order to understand the other person's perspective.

BE ABOUT YOUR FEELINGS
Assertive

THE WRONG WAY

- Resent the other person for having different thoughts and feelings.
- Speak harshly about the other person's feelings, causing him or her to resent you.
- Get back at the other person indirectly by withdrawing and pouting when he or she expresses feelings that oppose your own.

THE RIGHT WAY

- Become tolerant of the other person's viewpoint.
- State your feelings with tact and diplomacy.
- Express your viewpoint in a way that does not alienate the other person.

OVERCOME YOUR FEAR OF Rejection

THE WRONG WAY

- Fall apart when you hear something you don't like.
- Avoid any risk of rejection.
- Leave an issue unresolved because you fear that your opinion will be rejected.

THE RIGHT WAY

- Improve your self-esteem by empowering yourself to address the issue.
- Ask yourself, "What is the worst thing that could happen if I get rejected?"
- Ask yourself, "If I don't speak up, how will I feel about myself?"

DO SOMETHING TOGETHER EVERY DAY
Playful

THE WRONG WAY

- Avoid play because you just don't have time.
- Focus only on work.
- Wait for the "right time" to schedule something fun.

THE RIGHT WAY

- Make playtime with the other person a part of your routine.
- Realize that playing together enhances your relationship.
- Seize opportunities to bond through play.

TREAT THE OTHER PERSON WITH
Kindness

THE WRONG WAY

- Speak negatively to the other person.
- Hold on to negative thoughts about the other person.
- Treat the other person with less respect than you would a stranger.

THE RIGHT WAY

- Verbalize any positive thoughts so that you stay connected to the other person.
- Be kind so that the other person knows that you care.
- Display kindness in the midst of conflict.

GIVE CRITICISM IN A ᐱ WAY
Positive

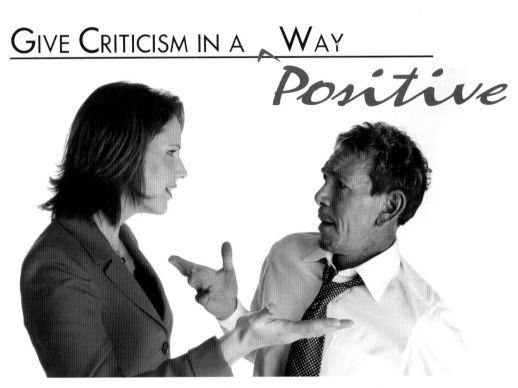

THE WRONG WAY

- Verbalize the faults of the other person.
- Criticize the other person without telling him or her something positive.
- Talk down to the other person.

THE RIGHT WAY

- Respect that the other person has a right to his or her thoughts and feelings, and know that you also have a right to what you think and feel.
- Always try to stay positive in your feedback, even when you have to say something negative. People are very sensitive to criticism.
- Find a way to keep the other person positive and hopeful. He or she will have a tendency to focus only on the negative things you say.

LEARN HOW TO CRITICISM
Receive

THE WRONG WAY

- Take everything personally so that you don't hear what is being said to you.
- Get defensive and fight back with blame and sarcasm.
- Attack the other person for his or her honest assessment.

THE RIGHT WAY

- Accept what is said to you in a calm manner.
- Try not to be too sensitive to the other person's opinion.
- Be aware that the feedback you are receiving could potentially help you improve yourself.

Take Control of Anger and Frustration

THE WRONG WAY

- Overreact and explode.
- Hold a grudge, and never forget what the other person has said or done to anger you.
- Hold anger in. This practice can lead to physical problems.

THE RIGHT WAY

- Express your frustration before it becomes anger.
- Express your feelings tactfully.
- Take a deep breath to calm down, and think before you speak.

LEARN TO LIKE
Yourself

THE WRONG WAY

- Blame the other person when you don't feel good about yourself.
- Expect the other person to make you happy.
- Be critical of yourself when your expectations are not met.

THE RIGHT WAY

- Accept your limitations as human.
- Focus on the positive, and talk to yourself about the good things in your life.
- Remember that mistakes are a basis for learning and not blame.

FIND WAYS WITH THE OTHER PERSON *to Laugh*

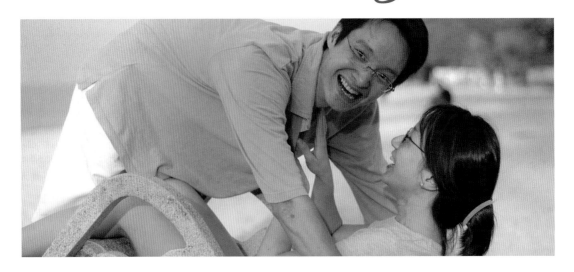

THE WRONG WAY

- Never take time to appreciate moments of joy.
- Take yourself so seriously that nothing is funny.
- Focus on the negative all the time.

THE RIGHT WAY

- Know that a good laugh is an energizing and bonding experience.
- Find situations to laugh at because they produce a physiological rush of positive feeling.
- Commit yourself to laughing each day to enhance overall well-being.

Schedule ^Time for the Two of You

TODAY

AM ·

·

·

PM ·

·

THE WRONG WAY

- Forget how special alone time is and fail to take it seriously.
- Stay focused on your own world to the exclusion of the other person.
- Get involved in only those activities that you enjoy, and forget about the other person's interests.

THE RIGHT WAY

- Recognize how valuable your time is with the other person.
- Schedule something special to show your commitment to the relationship.
- Choose an activity you know both of you will enjoy, and actively pursue it together.

DEVELOP OUTSIDE
Friendships

THE WRONG WAY

- Stay locked in your own little world.
- Believe that you can handle all your problems without the help of a friend.
- Assume that no one else could possibly understand what it's like to have your problems.

THE RIGHT WAY

- Work to develop friendships with people who share your interests.
- Make an effort to stay connected with friends.
- Treat your friends as you would treat a personal investment. The more you give, the more you get back.

DEVELOP OUTSIDE

Interests

THE WRONG WAY

- Put all of your energy into your work only.
- Assume you don't have time to pursue personal interests.
- Refuse to do anything without the other person.

THE RIGHT WAY

- Balance work and family with your own personal interests.
- Try something new, which makes you much more interesting to the other person.
- Do things on your own, and your level of confidence will increase.

SET ~ EXPECTATIONS
Realistic

THE WRONG WAY

- Demand that the other person do just as you say.
- Prevent the other person from expressing his or her point of view.
- Strive for a "perfect" relationship.

THE RIGHT WAY

- Try to accept the other person's faults, and forgive minor slights.
- Listen to the other person, and learn the reason for his or her point of view.
- Learn that while your relationship cannot be perfect, it can be really good. Strive for the latter.

LEARN TO *Forgive*

THE WRONG WAY

- Hold on to old wounds, which will make you bitter.
- Keep a scorecard of wrongdoings.
- Forget that you make mistakes, too.

THE RIGHT WAY

- Look at the big picture and ask if the problem is really serious.
- Let little wrongdoings go. They obscure what's really important in life.
- Think of the other person as a fallible human being who makes mistakes, just as you do.

16

FIND IN YOUR LIFE
Balance

THE WRONG WAY

- Put all of your energy into one area of your life.
- Ignore other options for happiness.
- Limit your possibilities by assuming you can't do something.

THE RIGHT WAY

- Focus on different areas of well-being, from physical to mental to spiritual.
- Spread your interests in different directions.
- Manage stress by directing it toward a passion.

Appreciate
THE OTHER PERSON

THE WRONG WAY

- Think of yourself first without regard to the other person.
- Only consider what is important to you, as if you are the most important person in the relationship.
- Take the other person for granted, and never express how much you appreciate him or her.

THE RIGHT WAY

- Verbalize your appreciation on a regular basis.
- Pay the other person compliments on a daily basis.
- Be specific about what you appreciate.

PRACTICE BEING

Optimistic

THE WRONG WAY

- Dwell on all the negative things that have happened in your relationship.
- Cut off all positive thoughts in order not to be disappointed later.
- Stay negative to keep the other person from being positive.

THE RIGHT WAY

- Ask yourself to think about three positive events that have happened in your relationship. Do this on a weekly basis.
- Challenge your negative thinking by focusing on the positives of each situation.
- Remember to seek out and enjoy positive experiences.

STAY *Committed*

THE WRONG WAY

20

- Abandon the relationship when you don't get your way.
- Move to a new relationship in hopes that it will be better.
- Expect a new relationship to be free of problems.

THE RIGHT WAY

- Be proactive to make positive changes when you don't like something about the relationship.
- Realize that you cannot have everything your way, and learn to compromise.
- Accept the other person, even with his or her faults.

OLD WOUNDS

Heal

THE WRONG WAY

- Never reconcile your differences with those who hurt you.
- Make your current relationship partner suffer because of your old wounds.
- Hold on to bitterness in order to avoid getting hurt again.

THE RIGHT WAY

- Face whatever hurt you experienced and deal with it directly.
- Learn to forgive those who hurt you by putting those incidents into perspective.
- Focus on the positive aspects of the present.

ENCOURAGE THE OTHER PERSON TO ⌃ISSUES
Discuss

THE WRONG WAY

- Cause the other person to shut down by criticizing his or her viewpoint.
- Discourage open communication by being judgmental.
- Act as if you don't care what the other person has to say.

THE RIGHT WAY

- Be tactful and diplomatic in your delivery to the other person.
- Show respect for his or her viewpoint.
- Encourage openness by staying positive even when you disagree with the other person.

MAKE IT TO TALK
Safe

THE WRONG WAY

- Criticize the other person's response.
- Explain to the other person why he or she is wrong instead of listening to him or her.
- Interpret what the other person is saying before he or she is finished talking.

THE RIGHT WAY

- Listen to what the other person says without interruption.
- Show the other person that you are listening by repeating what you understood him or her to have said.
- Tell the other person that you appreciate his or her honesty.

Recognize Your Fears

THE WRONG WAY

- Refuse to recognize the truth about yourself because you are afraid to do so.
- Refuse to admit that you are fallible.
- Deny that you have fears.

THE RIGHT WAY

- Be open to accepting and confronting your fears.
- Work on changing negative behaviors. This will help build your self-esteem and make you more capable of handling your fears.
- Remember that admitting your fears is the first step to overcoming them.

Work to Overcome Your Fear of *Change*

THE WRONG WAY

- Assume that you cannot avoid your basic fears.
- Avoid difficult decisions.
- Decide that you cannot change.

THE RIGHT WAY

- Commit to making small changes by focusing on the exact behavior that you wish to change.
- Remember to stay positive when you feel like you cannot overcome your fear.
- Ask yourself, "What is the worst thing that can happen?" when faced with a difficult decision.

RECOGNIZE YOUR SELF-TALK
^ Defeating

THE WRONG WAY

- Engage in negative thinking.
- Let negative thoughts outweigh positive ones.
- Allow negative thinking to become an automatic behavior.

THE RIGHT WAY

- Make an active effort to challenge and dispute negative thoughts.
- Do something proactive to redirect negative thoughts.
- Practice positive self-talk, and cultivate a positive attitude.

Determine Your Own *Needs*

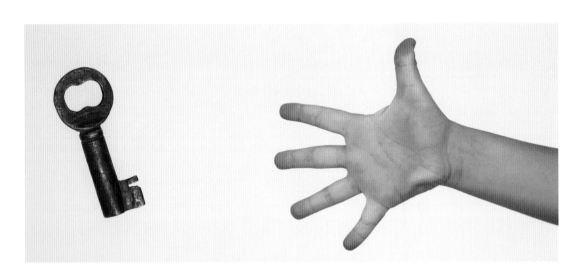

THE WRONG WAY

- Allow the other person's needs to come before your own.
- Let the other person determine what is best for you.
- Completely ignore your own needs.

THE RIGHT WAY

- Decide what you want in life and go after it.
- Learn to put your own needs first at least some of the time.
- Learn to do things that make you feel good about yourself.

PRACTICE REMINISCING ˄ THE OTHER PERSON
about How You Met

THE WRONG WAY

- Forget the past because all those memories don't count.
- Discount the things that brought you together because they happened in the past.
- Minimize the positives of the early part of the relationship because the negatives of the present seem more important.

THE RIGHT WAY

- Think about the reasons you got together. They are still important.
- Know that the other person and relationships constantly change, and be open to those changes.
- Determine how things have changed for the worse, and commit to doing something about it.

STAY
Physical

THE WRONG WAY

- Plop down in front of the TV or computer during all of your free time.
- Blame the other person for your boredom or lack of motivation.
- Watch other people live active lives and become jealous of them for being active.

THE RIGHT WAY

- Exercise with the other person to give you both that feeling of well-being.
- Regularly participate in an activity you both enjoy.
- Take care of the only body that you will ever have.

LEARN TO DISCUSS ⌃ TOPICS
Difficult

THE WRONG WAY

- Get angry at the other person instead of talking about issues rationally and directly.
- Avoid difficult topics because they make you feel uncomfortable.
- Refuse to listen because you don't want to hear anything that conflicts with what you believe.

THE RIGHT WAY

- Make it "safe" to talk without fear of being attacked.
- Be nonjudgmental as you listen to what the other person has to say.
- Verbally acknowledge the other person's viewpoints as valid.

Look Honestly at Your Own *Faults*

THE WRONG WAY

- Ignore your own problem areas as if they are not important.
- Deny that you have issues from your past that need to be addressed.
- Lie to yourself about the need to work on problem areas.

THE RIGHT WAY

- Recognize your faults.
- Have an active plan to change.
- Acknowledge and reward yourself when you make a positive change.

LEARN TO ACCEPT YOUR *Differences*

THE WRONG WAY

- Expect the other person to behave the way you want him or her to behave.
- Expect the other person to think just like you think.
- Be unforgiving of the other person's differences.

THE RIGHT WAY

- Accept the fact that all people are unique and will act differently.
- Develop empathy for the other person's differences.
- Understand that differences are important to a relationship, and learn to accept the other person the way he or she is.

LEARN TO BOUNDARIES
Set

THE WRONG WAY

- Allow the other person to define who you are.
- Allow the other person to determine what is important for you.
- Lose all sense of who you are.

THE RIGHT WAY

- Tell the other person what you want, and be assertive.
- Learn to say no.
- Let go of guilty thoughts by telling yourself that you have the right to think and feel as you do.

WORK TO OVERCOME YOUR FEAR OF *Conflict*

THE WRONG WAY

- Deny that you have any conflict in your relationship.
- Avoid conflict at any cost.
- Delay addressing conflict, and allow resentment to develop.

THE RIGHT WAY

- Face the uncomfortable feeling that conflict brings by telling yourself that an argument is only a conversation. Remember that facing your fear and addressing conflict raises your self-esteem.
- Always ask, "What is the worst thing that can happen if I speak up?"
- Understand that you will not only survive the conflict, you also will become stronger as a result of confronting the issues.

Maintain *Hope*

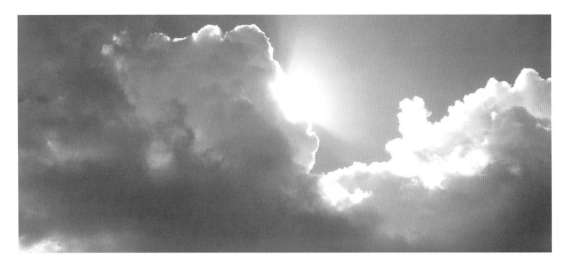

THE WRONG WAY

- Engage in negative self-talk.
- Let negative thinking become a habit.
- Do nothing, and let negativity take hold.

THE RIGHT WAY

- Practice being positive until it becomes part of your thinking.
- Recall examples of friends who have overcome discouragement, and model your actions after theirs.
- Find ways to keep hope alive.

Make Time for *You*

THE WRONG WAY

- Be afraid to say "no" because you fear you might disappoint your partner.
- Over-schedule yourself.
- Allow resentment to build because you do more for the other person than you do for yourself.

THE RIGHT WAY

- Say "no" when you know you just don't have the time (or desire) to do something.
- Schedule time alone to regroup and reenergize.
- Realize that you can be more helpful to the other person when you are in a calm, positive state of mind.

PRACTICE DURING DIFFICULT TIMES
Mental Toughness

THE WRONG WAY

- Give up quickly.
- Make no effort to correct what is wrong with the relationship.
- Let negative thoughts about the relationship guide you.

THE RIGHT WAY

- Focus on what is right in the relationship.
- Understand that commitment takes a lot of work.
- Focus on the fact that you have the courage to face your problems and do not run from the issues.

CONFRONT ABOUT YOUR RELATIONSHIP
Negative Thoughts

THE WRONG WAY

- Allow negative thoughts to dominate the relationship.
- Focus only on the negative aspects of the relationship.
- Allow negative thoughts to be automatic.

THE RIGHT WAY

- Challenge negative thoughts about the relationship by asking yourself what upsets you about the other person's behavior. Try to see the reason behind the other person's actions.
- Remind yourself of the positive aspects of your relationship.
- Replace negative thoughts with "at least" statements. For example, instead of thinking about how underappreciated you feel, tell yourself, "At least he/she does try to show appreciation by cooking a good dinner for me." This allows you to give the other person some credit for what he or she is doing right.

DEAL WITH
Denial

THE WRONG WAY

- Refuse to accept that you are in denial about your problems.
- Use denial as a way to avoid change.
- Allow denial to ruin your relationship.

THE RIGHT WAY

- Increase your self-esteem by confronting your problems.
- Take a risk to change those behaviors that you deny are problematic.
- Make yourself engage in behaviors you fear.

WORK ON ⌃ IN YOUR RELATIONSHIP

Boredom

THE WRONG WAY

- Blame the other person because you are bored.
- Fail to acknowledge that some boredom is normal.
- Accept that the relationship will continue to be boring.

THE RIGHT WAY

- Understand that it's natural to be bored some of the time.
- Realize that you have the power to make the relationship more exciting.
- Adopt new behavior and activities that will rejuvenate the relationship.

DEVELOP BETTER SKILLS

Listening

THE WRONG WAY

- Look away from the person or do something else while he or she is speaking.
- Interrupt or talk over the other person.
- Try to convince the other person that he or she is wrong.

THE RIGHT WAY

- Maintain eye contact while the other person is talking.
- Let the other person say what he or she has to say without interrupting him or her.
- Repeat back the other person's words so that he or she knows that you are listening.

MAKE YOURSELF

Heard

THE WRONG WAY

- Get defensive when the other person won't listen.
- Blame the other person for being a bad listener.
- Give up, and make no effort to confront the issue.

THE RIGHT WAY

- Find a way to speak so that the other person won't shut down or get defensive.
- Use a softer tone of voice when making a strong point.
- Choose words that are less accusatory when offering criticism.

FIGHT
Fairly

THE WRONG WAY

- Attack when you are hurt.
- Call the other person names.
- Try to "win" each fight.

THE RIGHT WAY

- Listen without interrupting.
- Let the other person vent so he or she will feel better, and remember that you have a right to do the same.
- Recognize that the other person's feelings are just as important as yours, and learn to compromise.

43

LEARN TO TAKE A *Time-Out* WHEN THINGS GET BAD

THE WRONG WAY

- Focus so much on the problems that you feel like ending the relationship.
- Blame the other person for all the difficulties, and accept none of the responsibility yourself.
- Forget the good aspects of the relationship because you think they don't count.

THE RIGHT WAY

- Take time away from the relationship to see both sides of the problem.
- Try and practice forgiveness if you are hurt by something the other person has done.
- Develop empathy for the other person by recognizing that there is a reason for his or her behavior.

Face HURT AND REJECTION

THE WRONG WAY

- Get angry and blame the other person when you are hurt.
- Refuse to let old wounds heal.
- Allow hurt and anger to build up, which can create physical and emotional problems.

THE RIGHT WAY

- Recognize that it is normal to feel hurt and rejected in life.
- Express your feelings of hurt and rejection in a tactful and diplomatic way.
- Try not to take the other person's feedback personally.

Learn to _Deal_ with Disappointment

THE WRONG WAY

- Deny that you are disappointed.
- Refuse to accept or deal with setbacks.
- Blame or lash out at the other person when you experience a setback or disappointment.

THE RIGHT WAY

- Tactfully verbalize your disappointment to the other person.
- Try not to let setbacks and disappointments overtake positive feelings.
- Accept the fact that you are disappointed, and develop a plan to deal with it.

Learn to Live in the *Moment*

THE WRONG WAY

- Always look to the future for happiness.
- Dwell on how happy you used to be.
- Remind the other person of mistakes he or she has made in the past.

THE RIGHT WAY

- Learn to appreciate present moments that bring joy.
- Create moments of happiness rather than waiting for something positive to happen.
- Appreciate something the other person has done for you today.

APPRECIATE ∧ TIMES
Quiet

THE WRONG WAY

48

- Constantly keep busy so you don't have to think about your relationship.
- Stay so busy with outside activities that you forget to make time for each other.
- Develop other activities that don't include the other person.

THE RIGHT WAY

- Learn to be "in the moment," and develop joy in quiet pursuits.
- Appreciate activities that involve only the two of you. Imprint these memories in your mind.
- Together develop a host of activities that are quiet in nature, like drinking coffee, playing games, or discussing good books.

Learn to Look at the Big Picture

THE WRONG WAY

- Focus on all of the little things the other person does wrong.
- Remember only the negative events in your life, and forget the positive.
- Magnify your partner's weaknesses and faults out of proportion.

THE RIGHT WAY

- Focus on meaningful qualities such as commitment and loyalty.
- Ask yourself if those minor slights are really that important.
- Try and realize that there are no perfect relationships; all of us are flawed.

SHARE A ⌃THAT KEEPS YOU BONDED
Spirituality

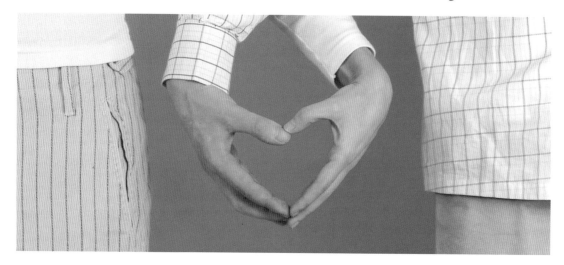

THE WRONG WAY

- Develop a cynicism toward faith, and avoid all contact with any house of worship.
- Vocalize to everyone why you are cynical about faith and worship.
- Stay negative about faith, and let that negativity guide everything that you do.

THE RIGHT WAY

- Develop a spirituality that guides you in order to deal better with stress.
- Share the same values as the other person in order to keep you closer with that person.
- Go to a house of worship, so that you can connect with the other person.

Take Risks with the Other Person

THE WRONG WAY

- Stay in a comfort zone where boredom is bound to occur.
- Let fear dictate your decisions.
- Complain that nothing ever gets better, and do nothing about it.

THE RIGHT WAY

- Engage in new behaviors to bring back the vibrancy to your relationship.
- Create new opportunities by taking risks.
- Reward yourself for making something new and different happen.

Richard Blue, PhD, has over thirty years of experience in the field of mental health. His career includes working with community mental health, acting as director of psychology at a psychiatric hospital, and currently keeping a solo practice in Atlanta, Georgia, where he specializes in relationship counseling. He has a weekly radio program on STAR 94.1 FM with which he reaches more than 100,000 listeners and helps callers deal with their relationship issues. He has also published numerous articles in his field. Dr. Blue is a diplomate of the American Board of Professional Psychologists (ABPP), and he won the Media Award for Presenting Psychology on the Radio from the Georgia Psychological Association in 2006.

about

Lisa Blue, PhD, JD, after earning her doctorate in psychology, counseled both individuals and families before turning to the practice of law. She joined the Dallas County District Attorney's office, where she tried more than 125 cases as a litigator for the misdemeanor, felony, and organized crime division. In 1985, Dr. Blue joined the law firm of Baron & Budd, PC. Specializing in environmental and toxic tort law, she has tried over 80 complex toxic tort civil cases to verdict. She became one of the firm's shareholders and has since been named one of "America's Top 50 Women Litigators" by *The National Law Journal* and "Trial Lawyer of the Year" by the Texas chapter of the American Board of Trial Advocates. A nationally recognized expert on jury selection, Dr. Blue has presented over 350 lectures to legal and university groups. Her numerous publications on jury selection and psychology include "Inside the Juror's Mind" and *ATLA's Blue's Guide to Jury Selection* (coauthored by Robert Hirschhorn).